Copyright © 2017 by Deborah Carter Mastelotto and Spellbound Publishers
All rights reserved

First published 2017

Manufactured in the United States

ISBN: 978-0-9977349-2-8

Library of Congress Control Number 2017932385

Notice: The information in this book is true and complete to the best of our knowledge. It is offered without guarantee on part of the author (Deborah Carter Mastelotto), Spellbound Publishers or Trailer Food Diaries, LLC. The author, Spellbound Publishers and Trailer Food Diaries, LLC disclaim all liability in connection with the use of this book.

All rights reserved. No part of this book may be reproduced or transmitted in any form whatsoever without prior written permission from the publisher except in case of brief quotations embodied in critical articles and reviews.

The Tarot Primer
Deborah Carter Mastelotto

PRAISE FOR THE TAROT PRIMER

"Deborah's Tarot class was the first time I was introduced to the basics of Tarot. I feel like it could have been very overwhelming, however with The Tarot Primer and Deborah's way of explaining everything it was fun and educational. The book was laid out in a perfect way to understand the meanings of the cards and then how they all flow together. Since I am very new to this, if I had gone home without the book it would have been hard to remember everything I had learned at the class. It was so easy to be able to lay out the cards and then reference each card meaning and how they flow together with the book at home. Great book! I will be using it for a long time!"
- Angela Pruitt

"I was so impressed by how clear and simple Deborah's book made everything seem. She is such a great teacher, and the class so enjoyable."- S. Easton

"As a beginner and someone who didn't know the first thing about Tarot, I thought I would take Deborah's class, understand Tarot a little bit, take my cards out every now and then and have fun. Instead, I dove in and fell in love. I am still amazed at everything I learned in the three hours of her class. Having her book as a reference during class worked so well for me. I felt able to understand quickly what Tarot cards say, how to read them and understand what they mean. To quote from her book "the cards have no agenda" and for me, that is important to remember. I enjoy reading and interpreting the cards. I know this is something I will have in my life from now on and I thank you for introducing Tarot to me. Looking forward to the next class." - C. Dunlap

"It's really the best Tarot book I've ever used." - M. Staffa

DEDICATION

This book is dedicated to people everywhere on a quest to become their own oracle.

TABLE OF CONTENTS

Foward..11
Tarot 101..15
How to Use Tarot Cards.......................................25
The Minor Arcana...37
    Aces..41
    Twos...43
    Threes..45
    Fours..47
    Fives...49
    Sixes...51
    Sevens..53
    Eights..55
    Nines..57
    Tens..59
Court Cards..61
    Kings 65
    Queens...…69
    Knights...75
    Pages..81
The Major Arcana 87
Spreads..113
A Final Word...127
Notes...130

FORWARD

WHY DO YOU NEED THIS BOOK?

It's true, the Tarot is a deep and complex oracle and it can take years to explore every nuance. You're curious about the Tarot and you have to start somewhere, so where do you begin? I've observed a tendency in instructional Tarot books towards complexity. Sometimes I think authors begin with the assumption they need to tell you every detail about the Tarot right off the bat. These details can be confusing to a beginner who may never have handled Tarot cards before, or even had a Tarot reading. Additionally, most books on the market are written for unique and specific

FORWARD

decks so can't easily be used as a general starting point with any other Tarot deck. You can do what I did when I first began my journey with the Tarot, struggle through the Tarot books available and try to teach yourself, a long and painful process. You can track down a Tarot teacher and take classes, fun, but not always available. Or, you can read this book to get a very basic but clear understanding and dive in. Read all those other books later when they make more sense to you. This little book gives you enough simple information to begin using any Tarot deck you choose in about three hours. Of course, like with anything, the more practice you have with the Tarot the better you become and the more fun you'll have. You have to start somewhere. This book is only the beginning.

TAROT 101

Some say an oracle is a method or vehicle to predict the future. Some say divination could be a person, object, or even a place offering answers to questions posed to it. Oracles have been part of human society since the beginning of time. Ancient Chinese scholars heated turtle shells and interpreted the cracks. Farmers consult almanacs to determine the best time to plant, fashion designers forecast the next trend by watching young people on the street, and politicians trust important decisions to focus groups and experts.

Everyone needs an oracle of some kind, at sometime or another. Often all we need is a new perspective. Sometimes our unconscious knows the answer but we are unable to easily access it. Sometimes we need a vehicle to help us get past the barrier of our own ego, to help us get out of our own way, to get to the truth. Sometimes we just need to see the answer in brightly colored pictures, which leads us to Tarot cards.

WHAT ARE TAROT CARDS?

A Tarot deck consists of 78 cards, usually a little (or a lot) larger than traditional playing cards. Tarot cards are a way of accessing our personal intuition and can often provide objective, visual and tangible advice. The pictures on the cards speak to every human, no matter their country or language. The cards have no agenda. They are free of any attachments or previous prejudices. They are innocuous and clean, ready for you to use in whatever way works for you as long as you stay mindful and handle them with love in your heart.

Tarot cards reflect what is going on inside of your head and your life. They are always about you, the questioner or "querent." Even if they suggest other people or situations, they do it from the perspective of how these things impact you. Please try not to argue with them. Do not whine or obsess about a negative answer. If you do not like a card you draw, rearrange your head into a calmer state, then try again.

The cards, and the words on the cards, have no power in themselves at all. They are merely a way for your unconscious mind to communicate with your conscious mind. The goal is to try and make that path from subconscious to conscious as smooth and obstacle-free as possible. It's easier than you might think.

The best frame of mind while asking questions and drawing cards is peace. The more peaceful and positive your state of mind, the more likely a peaceful, positive outcome with the cards. This is true of life as well, isn't it? If the cards give you some favorable advice, you can relax -- you actually knew what to do all along. If the cards seem negative, put them away and try again. Things change. This is a physics principle.

ORIGIN OF TAROT

No one knows the exact origin of Tarot cards. Some believe they were once pages of a book used to teach all facets of esoteric knowledge and provide advice about how to handle daily life experiences. When society turned against any practitioners of the esoteric arts, divination (and oracles) fell out of favor and became risky to practice. One theory is the pages of those books were separated and disguised as a card game. The earliest known version of the current 78-card Tarot decks dates back to Italy during the fifteenth century and is the ancestor of the modern playing cards we use today.

MINOR ARCANA

Arcana consists of fifty-six cards, and are divided into two groups: twenty-two Major Arcana, and fifty-six Minor Arcana.

They are also divided into four suits, numbered ace through ten. They depict elements of every day life. You will also find four court cards per suit (Page, Knight, Queen and King) as opposed to the three found in traditional playing cards (Knight, Queen, King). Some Tarot decks deviate from this formula, and that's fine, but this formula is the one we use in this book to make learning easy.

The four suits of the Minor Arcana are Swords (traditionally Spades in playing card decks), Cups (traditionally Hearts in playing card decks), Wands (traditionally Clubs in playing card decks) and Pentacles or Coins (traditionally Diamonds in playing card decks). Each suit also depicts the four elements: Swords for Air, Cups for Water, Wands for Fire, and Pentacles or Coins for Earth. The more of these "suit" cards you find in your reading, the more you are in control of the outcome of your current situation.

MAJOR ARCANA

The Major Arcana of the tarot depict universal archetypes and various stages of spiritual development. These cards let you know when you're approaching something significant, sometimes a situation outside of your control, sometimes even a turning point for your soul's growth. In this case they can also show you, in pictures, the right way to handle the situation.

The illustrations on the cards incorporate various symbols, which help you to interpret the meaning of the card. Many of these symbols have an astrological, alchemical or numerological origin and our unconscious mind identifies with them. Call it Jung's "Collective Unconscious Memory", or "Universal Consciousness" or something else you like better. It doesn't matter whether you can find an acceptable explanation or not, Tarot cards work.

For whatever reason, your unconscious mind is familiar with these symbols, so trust your first instinctual feelings about them. If the history of the Tarot interests you, there are many good books available for further study.

WHY USE TAROT CARDS?

Tarot cards are a vivid, compelling way to see where you are. They can reveal what you did, what you are doing now and how you feel about that, as well as the potential of these actions in the past, right now, and a few months in the future. They can give you fresh insights into your options. Cards are event-specific and people-specific. They can give guidance as to possible obstacles and probable outcomes if you do not change your course of action. You can sometimes change your Tarot readings (and probable outcomes) by changing your mind.

CAN ANYONE READ THE TAROT?

Some say it's a gift to be able to read Tarot cards and are in awe of those who do it. Others say almost anyone can be taught to read Tarot cards. A great chef once told me, "Anyone can cook if the desire is present" and I feel the same way about reading the Tarot. We all carry the necessary information in our subconscious mind to live our lives correctly, but years of conditioning submerges our intuition and replaces our intuitive decision making with fact collecting. The Tarot allows each of us to bypass that conditioning and access our intuitive mind again. Similar to physical exercise, the more you practice with Tarot cards, the easier it becomes because you are building up your intuitive "muscle." This way, through practice, we each can be our own oracles with using a simple deck of Tarot cards.

HOW TO USE TAROT CARDS

Placing shuffled or mixed Tarot cards in a particular order is called a 'throw' or 'layout', but before you try any throw or layout, you need to meet your cards. You might even need to spend some time alone with your cards, especially at first. If your cards are new, take them out of their original box or wrapping. If your cards have been used by someone else, you should probably 'clear' them (see number two below under "Here's what I think is important" on page 26).

First, meet your cards.

Remove the first two or three identification cards or instruction cards and lay them aside as well as any book included with them. For right now you won't need the book included with your cards.

Now pick up your pack. Take the first card and really look at it. Say the name of the card out loud as you hold it in your hand, like 'Ace of Wands' or 'The Fool'. Go through the entire deck, one by one, card by card, saying the name of each card out loud to yourself. Take your time.

Notice the color, the pattern, the number or Roman numeral. Each card has something to say: either a few words of advice, some strong suggestions, or a description of a mood or person. Eventually you will have a key phrase for every card in your deck, but right now you are just meeting each other.

Notice if any of the 'people' cards (court cards in the Minor Arcana) remind you of anyone. Notice how the other cards make you feel. Happy? Sad? Anxious? Notice if you take an instant dislike to a particular card or find yourself drawn to any other. Do this to every card slowly, until you get to the last card in your deck.

Now, shuffle or mix your deck. Use any way that feels comfortable for you. Because the cards in many Tarot decks are oversized some find them difficult to shuffle in the traditional way. Please don't worry about style, this isn't Las Vegas. The important thing is to mix and mix and mix until your energy is all over each card and you find yourself in an almost Zen-like mental state. At first your cards will feel stiff and difficult to shuffle but as you work you will notice an almost softening of the cards. This is what you want. Some readers even put a deck of new cards in bed with them for a month. This may be a bit extreme for you, but no matter what your method, the more you work with them the easier shuffling or mixing them will be. Practice makes perfect.

You can even place all the cards face down on a table or even the floor and mix them all up using both hands. Just be sure all the cards remain face down. The method you use to mix your cards isn't as important as finding a method that is easy enough for you to do frequently.

THROWING THE CARDS.
Begin by taking all the cards from their box.

Relax and center yourself. Remove any distractions. Turn the ringer off to your phone or better yet, put it in another room. Close your eyes and take one or two deep breaths. Try not to be overwhelmed when you first begin to use your cards. Keep it simple and just shuffle, shuffle, shuffle. Cut. Shuffle. Throw out three, call out their names, collect the cards and put them back with the other cards and shuffle, shuffle, shuffle, repeat. Easy.

Do not worry about 'losing' a reading. Collect your cards after a throw and put them back in the deck. Now do it again.

I've worked with some amazing Tarot teachers, attended Tarot classes and seminars, read hundreds of books and articles. Many suggest a long involved ceremony before throwing Tarot cards. Some place crystals on the four corners of the tables, draw circles and symbols, recite invocations, etcetera, etcetera. And some really need a ceremony to clear their heads and focus. I'm sure that's fine for them, but this book is for the rest of us who aren't comfortable with that stuff..

If you like a ceremony to get your mind to the right state, I'm not judging. But this book is for the rest of us who do not. I've spent many an enjoyable afternoon sitting in the middle of my bed, or at my kitchen table, drinking wine with a friend and throwing Tarot cards. We used no ceremony besides the pleasant company of friendship and the readings were still spot on.

Here's what I think is important:

1. HONOR THE FOUR ELEMENTS.

The importance of honoring the four elements has long been understood in many cultures, so I recommend doing it, too. I use a candle to honor the element of fire, incense for the element of air, stones and/or crystals for earth and some sort of liquid to honor water. When I do readings for clients I always have a glass of water for each of us at hand, a small bowl of my favorite rocks, a candle burning somewhere and either incense or sage. Try to use only natural scents.

2. CLEANSE AND SHUFFLE THE CARDS.

The purpose of cleansing the cards is to clear the energy field around the deck, especially if the deck had a previous owner or it has been handled by many people. I've read and seen and used so many different ways of cleansing cards I would not blame any of you for feeling confused.

There are many ways to do this:

1. Wave a wand of burning sage around the cards.

2.Seal your cards in a zip lock baggie and freeze them over night.

3.Let your cards sit in moonlight during a full moon. I prefer this simple technique to cleanse cards: Before you begin your session, take your whole pack and straighten each card so they are all facing the same way.

After I have done that, I knock once on the back of the deck and say "clear", wrap them in silk (always silk) and place a bar of selenite on top of them. Selenite is a lovely white translucent stone, good for clearing things and easy to find at most crystal shops.

PRO TIPS:
If I want to really do a major clearing, like I do after working an event where lots of people have handled my cards, I actually sort them out in order, Ace to King, suit by suit, including the major Arcana from 'The Fool' to 'The World'.

I wrap my cards in a silk scarf and put them in a pretty wooden box when I'm not using them, but I also carry a deck in my purse. That deck lives a silk bag with a piece of selenite. That's it.

Say "Thank You" every time. Every. Time. I can't emphasize the importance of daily gratitude, and gratitude before and during any important undertaking.

Shuffle the cards often, even when you aren't doing a reading. It's good for you. Not only does shuffling and mixing cards act as a meditation but it's also good exercise for the intuitive area of your mind: your pineal gland.

3. CHOOSE THE CARDS.
A number of cards are chosen and laid out in some kind of order, called a spread. You can either take these cards straight from the top of your freshly mixed deck or chosen randomly from a pile after mixing. It's up to you.

HOW TO USE TAROT CARDS

There are as many different ways to choose your cards as there are spreads to choose from. You can take them from the top of your pile. You can fan them out and intuitively choose your cards from the fanned cards. You can cut the deck and pull the card on the bottom. You can even spread your cards out all over a table and pick your cards that way, or any way you like.

The most popular spreads use between three and twelve cards. The position of the card in most spreads indicates a specific part of the question. For example, the left card of a three-card layout can be past, the center card is the present, and the right hand card would be the probable future.

The first layout should be a daily one, like a meditation. Clear the deck, then shuffle, shuffle, shuffle while you ask yourself, "What kind of day will I have today", shuffle, shuffle. Lay three cards face down in no particular order (don't look!) and throw a silk scarf over them. Then go live your day.

HOW TO USE TAROT CARDS

At the end of your day, pull off the silk scarf and turn over your cards. Repeat the name of each card and the key phrase you have associated with it. (I help teach key phrases for each card later in this book). Think about each card and how they describe your day, the people you encountered, and the nature of your interactions. Later, when you feel adventurous, try some of the three card spreads in the back of this book.

Eventually you will want to be immediate and instinctive with your cards, so you will try to memorize a key phrase or two for each card. This way the phrase and a corresponding meaning pops into your mind each time you see that card.

It is important to keep in mind any first feelings you have about each card before you know anything about them. These first feelings are important, so even if the books you read tell you one interpretation of a card (or twenty), the feeling you got intuitively, even if it's a different meaning from the meaning in the book, is the most important meaning. That card may always hold that meaning for you.

That is why Tarot books all have so many different meanings for each card, to the point of confusing the issue. Each author tries to include as many different versions and meanings as possible. Just remember: the only important meaning is the meaning you assign. For this reason I do not suggest any Tarot books for you at first. Except this one, of course.

The deck you choose is your deck, these are your cards, and these will be your meanings. Sometimes the most frustrating readings I do are for people who know a little about the Tarot and interpret as I throw the cards. Invariably their meanings are not my meanings. Trust your first instincts. This is what reading the Tarot is all about.

THE MINOR ARCANA

The Minor Arcana, or "lesser secrets," generally describe events, situations, or people related to our everyday life. If your throw includes many cards from the Minor Arcana, this indicates a situation within your personal control. The Minor Arcana can show us what is really going on with us, even to the point of calling us out on our own self-delusion. So if we pay attention, the Minor Arcana can show us practical ways to manage the things that happen to us on a daily basis.

The fifty-six cards in the Minor Arcana are divided into four suits: Wands (or Rods or Staves), Cups, Swords and Pentacles (or Coins or

Discs). Each of these suits stands for a particular approach to life. Each Minor Arcana suit has a distinct quality all its own and corresponds to the four elements: Fire, Water, Air and Earth. Our everyday experiences are always a blend of these elements, but sometimes you feel one element more acutely than the others, or a situation is more one element than another. Count the elements in your throw. Just doing that alone can sometimes give you an answer. When you look at your Tarot spreads in terms of the elements, your Tarot readings will show you how and where to balance things out. For example: if you see many Cups in your reading, the issue you are facing is an emotional one, possibly concerning your relationships. They may be suggesting you become more grounded before making decisions.

SUITS OF THE MINOR ARCANA

Wands - Fire - The Physical

Wands are always creativity, action and movement. Wands describe enthusiasm, impulsivity, adventure, risk-taking and confidence. This suit corresponds to the yang or masculine principle in Chinese philosophy. This energy flows outward and generates forward motion and passionate involvement. Lots of Wands in a reading indicate lots of action and activity.

Cups - Water - The Emotional

Cups represent emotions, feelings, and Spirit. They describe inner states and relationships. Cups energy flows inward. Cups correspond to the yin, or feminine principle in Chinese philosophy. Many Cups in a reading indicate lots of emotions and feelings, or the subject in question is a personal one, not business.

Swords - Air - The Intellectual

Swords are thoughts, words, and reason; spoken, written or silent. Swords are also associated with disharmony and unhappiness. Swords encourage our intellect to decide our course of action, but too many Swords in a reading indicate troubles, possible difficulties, hard words, or a cranky disposition at the time of the reading. Sit quietly holding the cards and see if you can find your happy place. When you feel more neutral, throw the cards again to see which cards are still in your reading.

Discs, Pentacles, or Coins - Earth - The Material
Discs are all about practicality, security and material concerns. They are your physical experiences, work, prosperity and wealth of all kinds, also either earning or spending. Many Discs almost always indicate money or work issues, even if this isn't the question you asked.

NUMBERED CARDS OF THE MINOR ARCANA
The suits are structured like our everyday playing cards with ten numbered cards (Ace-Ten).

ACES

All of the Aces represent beginning energy. They are the purist energy of their suit. An Ace always announces something new and is always positive. They are the best cards in any suit. New beginnings and possibilities, opportunity, potential, ideas, inspiration and that which is about to happen. Even one Ace in your reading indicates something new is coming. Many Aces indicate an important situation is about to begin involving most, if not all, the elements.

Ace of Wands: "A new course of action."
Creative force, enthusiasm, courage, confidence, fertility, sex, a new art project, a decision or an idea to move in a new direction. With the Ace of Discs or Coins, an indicator of a new job.

Ace of Cups: "A new powerful emotion or love."
Emotional force, intuition, intimacy, harmony, a new love affair with something or someone, (especially with the Two of Cups). If paired with The

Lovers card, it could foretell the beginning of a significant relationship.

Ace of Swords: "A new idea, contract or plan."
Mental force, truth, justice, a new contract. A brilliant idea, a new plan, especially with an Ace of Wands, this can indicate a new plan of action.

Ace of Discs or coins: "New work project or money opportunities."

Material force, prosperity, a new money making idea or job. If the eight of discs is also in the reading, a learning curve is indicated. If it includes the three of discs, it's a new project you already have the skills to handle.

THE MINOR ARCANA

TWOS

Twos are always about choices or an attempt to find a balance. They are about union, partnership, and decisions. Many twos in a reading indicate juggling many projects, many choices and/or decisions, a reconciliation or reunion. Think in terms of possible partnerships.

Two of Wands: "The choice between security and Adventure."

You have what you need, and yet you yearn for something more. Personal power but hesitation. Boldness, originality. Success in business but a desire for more. Constant striving never satisfied.

Two of Cups: "The choice to love."

Balance in a relationship, attraction, connection, truce. A new relationship, especially with an Ace of Cups.

Two of Swords: "The choice to retreat from argument."

Blocked emotions, avoidance, stalemate, agree to disagree. Shelving the discussion for later (or never).

Two of Discs: "The choice of work projects."
Balancing aspects of life, juggling, flexibility, working on several projects at once, multiple streams of income. A choice between two equally attractive jobs.

THREES

Threes indicate a strong expression of the suit, or break in the stalemate. Creativity, opportunities or something created from the energy of the two's of its suit. Multiple threes in a reading can indicate group activities or situations involving more than one person. Threes indicate a fork in the road where a decision must be made, which sometimes brings uncertainty and confusion with it.

Three of Wands: "Waiting for your ship to come in."

Lots of action. Historically, the merchant classes were into shipping. Visualize packing your ship with goods and sending it off, awaiting its return bringing your profits. This card indicates much planning for a trip or project but a wait for fruition. Exploration, good business acumen, an opportunity to act. Travel, especially in conjunction with The Chariot.

Three of Cups: "Lots of Love. A party. More than two in a relationship."

Lots of love? Exuberance, friendship, community. A group of girls. Possibly more than two in a relationship. Infidelity, especially when drawn with the Three of Swords and/or Seven of Swords.

Three of Swords: "The broken heart card."

Lots of sorrow? Infidelity, sadness, disappointment, an argument, a possible ending to a relationship.

Three of Discs: "Lots of work experience."

Lots of work? Mozart card. This card describes being really good at what you do. Leading a team.

FOURS

Fours indicate a 'time out.' Fours are structure, stability, orderliness and practicality, complacency, and satisfaction. Many fours in a reading indicate fruition or a foundation.

Four of Wands: "House party!"
Take time out for a celebration. Freedom, excitement, happy home. This card often indicates the home itself, an actual house, or staying in.

Four of Cups: "Unsure of what you want."
Time out to evaluate feelings. Boredom. Hesitation to try something new, apathy, self-absorption, going within. It's there for you, but you have to reach for it.

Four of Swords: "Time out."
A pause before the fruition of a plan, or the need for a break. Time out for a much-needed break. Rehabilitation. Rest, contemplation, quiet preparation, illness, or recovery from illness, vacation time.

Four of Discs: "Holding tight to money or possessions."

Time out from spending. Some call this the 'Miser' card. Possessiveness, control, saving money, budgeting, refusing to share resources.

›
FIVES

The Fives indicate conflict, difficulties and hard times. Hard times motivate us to change something, to make adjustments, especially adjustments in our attitudes. The element of the Five gives us insight to where we need the adjustment. Loss, regret, conflict, difficult choices, challenges. in a reading, many fives indicate being stuck in a negative attitude and drastic need to change.

Five of Wands: "Hard times with conflicts."
A wrestling match, disagreement, competition, hassles but nothing serious. A suggestion to stop starting arguments over nothing.

Five of Cups: "Hard times with sad memories."
Sad memories get in the way of enjoying the present. An adjustment is needed to look forward to a positive future. Let go of what you've lost and embrace what you have. Loss, bereavement, regret. Sad memories. An adjustment in feelings is

needed to move forward.

Five of Swords: "Conflict with a bully."
Hard times with a bully. A humiliating defeat. A battle between unequal opponents, open dishonor. Someone's communication and behavior need to change—it might be you.

Five of Discs: "Hard times with money."
A poverty consciousness, may be magnified by attitude. A need to realize financial help may be more spiritual than physical. A change in attitude is needed to embrace abundance. Help is available but you can't or won't see it. Ill health, rejection, fear of poverty. Financial help is more spiritual than physical.

SIXES

Sixes represent generosity and somewhat unequal relationships, and one person standing out or helping someone else. You may be the helper or the one being helped. Sixes are sweetness, and old friendships. In general, Sixes are good. Many Sixes in a reading indicate positive adjustments in thoughts, attitudes or conditions.

Six of Wands: "Generosity with public recognition."
Triumph, acclaim, pride, public recognition, heroism. A promotion or raise.

Six of Cups: "Generosity with friendships."
A blast from the past, old friends, acts of kindness, innocence, childhood, children.

Six of Swords: "Generosity with help."
Recovery after rough times, travel, help through a tough period.

Six of Discs: "Generosity with money."

Sharing with someone/accepting help from someone: resources, knowledge, power, money.

SEVENS

Solitary action, or the contemplation of action. In a reading, many sevens indicate a period of introspection or solitude before taking action, especially with The Hermit card. Handling projects alone."

Seven of Wands: "Me against the world."
Solitary action. A feeling of doing battle alone, a need to handle things on your own. Aggression, defiance, conviction in spite of the odds against you, winning against the odds. Help may be offered but not wanted.

Seven of Cups: "Too many choices."
Solitary choice. Trying to choose but unable to decide. Wishful thinking, imagination, fantasy, options.

Seven of Swords: "Dishonesty."
Theft, lying, solitary duplicity, running away, taking more than the fair share, sneaky behavior.

Someone is being deceitful -- it may be you. Can also represent lying to oneself. When drawn with the Three of Cups this can indicate unfaithfulness.

Seven of Discs: "Patience."
Solitary waiting. The harvest is almost ready, waiting for a hard-earned reward, assessment, a rest after hard work.

EIGHTS

Eights are associated with all kinds of movement and usually represent a challenge to be faced and overcome. Many eights indicate a positive change of mind, status, or action by overcoming many challenges.

Eight of Wands: "It's happening fast!"
The challenge to be faced and overcome is about action and speed of action. It's almost here! Quick action, speed, conclusion, news.

Eight of Cups: "Walk away and don't look back."
The challenge to be faced and overcome is emotional. Leaving an old way for a new way, non-confrontational ending, moving on, a life change, moving house. Leaving an old set of friends. Divorce or separation. Quitting or changing a job.

Eight of Swords: "A prison of your own making."
The challenge to be faced and overcome is mental. A feeling of powerlessness, restriction, confu-

sion. You feel stuck, but what you think is holding you back is not real. There is a way out but you cannot (or will not) see it.

Eight of Discs: "Learning something new."
The challenge to be faced and overcome is professional. Doing something over and over again to perfect it, learning a new skill, diligence, acquiring knowledge, attention to detail. A new job or school. A learning curve.

NINES

Intensity, growth through experience, the element of the suit to a high degree. Many Nines in a reading indicate situations or events are heating up and almost nearing completion. Persevering under pressure. Holding on despite resisiting forces. Another plateau awaits.

Nine of Wands: "A lot on your plate but you can handle it."
Almost too much action. Success with a heavy workload. Over-committing. Biting off almost more than you can chew. Perseverance, stamina in the face of an almost overwhelming task, a feeling of being overburdened.

Nine of Cups: "The Wish Card."
Almost too much of a good thing. You get your wish! But the thing desired may not be as great as you expected. You got what you wanted, but now what? Get clear about what you want because it's coming. Satisfaction of a secret longing. Sensual pleasure, reward.

Nine of Swords: "The insomnia card."

Almost too much thinking. Worry keeps you up at night, difficulties mostly in the mind, bad dreams, guilt, worry.

Nine of Discs: "You have everything you want or need on your own."

Almost too much prosperity. The card of self-satisfaction and self-reliance. Bills paid, food on the table, now you can get creative. All is right with the world, successful single life, refinement. Possibly a bird in a gilded cage.

TENS

The ultimate of each suit. Excess, or completion. Many tens in a reading can indicate endings, which will soon transform into new beginnings.

Ten of Wands: "Ultimate effort."
Overextending, heavy burdens, a struggle but the worst is almost over, being weighed down with tasks, taking the lion's share of the responsibility in a relationship, uneven distribution of duties.

Ten of Cups: "Ultimate happiness."
The 'happy family' card. Joy, peace, abundance, family love.

Ten of Swords: "Ultimate unhappiness."
Bottoming out, victim mentality, martyrdom, misery, true grief.

Ten of Discs: "Ultimate finances."
Either receiving it or paying it out. Financial prosperity. Inheritance, insurance payout, a big check.

COURT CARDS

Court Cards can be tricky because they can have multiple meanings, but for now let's think of Court Cards as people like you and me, your brother or sister, boss, husband, wife, or parent. The Court Cards shouldn't be isolated, or read separately. Like us, Court Cards need to be in contact with each other and with the other cards. They live in our environment, like we do. If they pop up in your reading they have popped up in your life, or will. "Who is this person and what are they doing here?" is the question we ask when a Court Card shows up in our readings. Look to the cards surrounding the Court Cards: they tell you how they interact with the querent.

COURT CARDS

The easiest way to learn Court Cards is to connect the ones that pop up in your readings to a specific person in your life. For instance, you get a King of Cups, so you say to yourself, oh, The King of Cups—the 'Uncle Bob' card. It may not represent actual Uncle Bob in this reading, but I promise you, it is someone like him in some way.

And just to make things a bit more complicated, here are a couple of secondary meanings of Court Cards:

- An aspect of a personality.
- An aspect of a situation or the way you or someone else may be or should be acting in a specific situation. They can be a suggestion to modify the personality of the querent to better serve the situation.

Only after I've exhausted all possible real person meanings in a reading do I go on to explore secondary meanings for Court Cards. And even when I do go to secondary meanings, time eventually proves it was a person after all. You could go on happily reading your own cards, and everyone else's, for years without ever learning secondary meanings and I think they complicate things for the beginning reader. So we start with easy.

COURT CARDS AS SIGNIFICATORS

The easiest first thing to learn is which Court Card represents you. So pay close attention to the descriptions of each card. One of the descriptions will resonate with you. It doesn't have to be a perfect fit, but you will feel a kinship to one of the Court Cards.

Once I was in New Orleans and got a reading from a guy in a tiny tarot shop. He had maybe, fifty decks on shelves all around him and he chose which deck to use for my reading based on which Court Card I most closely resembled physically. I remember nothing of the actual reading, but that little trick stayed with me. The Court Card you identify with is your 'significator.' You see it pop up time and time again, as a gentle reminder to remember who you are.

COURT CARDS

As soon as you figure out which card best represents you, you can then move on to the next, most significant adult in your life and find a card identity for them too. It's a process, but it's fun.

Court Cards with Wands are impulsive, physically active and charming.

Court Cards with Cups are gentle, sweet, artistic and a little passive/aggressive.

Court Cards with Swords are smart and can take your head off any time they aren't pleased.

Court Cards with Discs are stable financially, or are working on it. Money is a big deal to these guys.

COURT CARDS

THE KINGS

He may be a significant person in your life, or someone you just met or will meet. Kings are husbands, older brothers, fathers, grandfathers, teachers, counselors or bosses. Usually they are older, but they can also be young men who are married and/or taking on a lot of responsibility.

The King of Wands
the King of Wands is pure Fire energy, and because of this he might be an Aries, Leo or Sagittarius man. He's energetic, adventurous and very charming. He can talk anyone into anything and people follow him wherever he leads. He's a physically active, masculine man. People are always impressed with the King of Wands, especially at first meeting. He is usually good with business, but not always stable financially because he likes to take risks that keep his finances fluctuating. But, he's a lucky guy and usually comes out on top. He's a natural born leader, a visionary,

and a master at delegating and inspiring his team. He likes a challenge and gets a rush from change for the sake of change. He often has or had light hair.

The King of Cups
the King of Cups is pure passive Water energy. He is a perfect example of combining the masculine and the feminine. He could be a Pisces, Cancer or Scorpio. This is a guy who is definitely in touch with his feminine side. He is a man of music art, poetry and sometimes he doesn't have a 'real' job. Quite often he drinks a bit. He's sweet, usually kind and considerate, sensitive, and creative. He's not a strong disciplinarian, and prefers to be seen as the loving one, leaving the hard stuff for others to do. He's usually a good listener, diplomatic, and almost always ready to lend a helping hand to those in need. He usually means well, but he can be a little flaky and not good at follow through. If he isn't your father, he's like a kindly father figure. He's more creative and sensitive than practical and he's the most loving of all the

kings. His feelings are more important to him than facts.

The King of Swords

The King of Swords is pure Air energy, so he may be a Gemini, Libra or Aquarius man. He is the kind of guy who puts his faith in facts and the power of his own intellect. He's usually a socially powerful guy, though not necessarily an extrovert. He likes and respects authority, especially his own. He's a bit judgmental and is something of a micro-manager. He's not good at delegating—he believes he can accomplish everything on his own. He's not afraid of hard work but would rather work with his brain than his hands. He gives good advice, especially financial, but he tends to be conservative. He keeps his emotions under tight control. He may be a judge, lawyer, doctor, military or a businessman and often has dark hair. He can seem detached, opinionated and possibly too forceful. He is not impressed by glamour. He expects the facts and the force of his ideas and words to be absolute.

The King of Discs

The King of Discs or Coins (or Pentacles) is the pure, solid power of Earth. He may be a Taurus, Virgo or Capricorn man, or another sign but possessing the same earthy qualities. He's a stable family man who loves his children passionately and is serious about financial security. He's proud of what he has accomplished and accumulated, and loves to create a stable world for his loved ones. He lives for the opportunity to take care of others, though he's no push-over or easy touch when it comes to money. He's the guy you go to for good, practical advice. He is a little old-fashioned and gets his self worth from the financial stability he's acquired. He's not struggling to make ends meet at this stage of his life, no matter his social class. He's not necessarily a leader and in fact, leading is not as important to him as what he gains in the long run. He's a planner and a great manager. He's not spontaneous and he doesn't like change at all.

COURT CARDS

THE QUEENS

Queens are adult females, living or not. They're either a part of your life now or you will soon meet them. They could even have an impact on your life without you ever meeting them. Queens can be you, someone you work for or with, your mother, grandmother, sister, or any other women in a position to affect your life either casually or profoundly. Queens are changeable, and can have a far-reaching effect by their connections and influences to Kings, Knights and other Queens. Think of the game of chess. The entire game is about protecting the King, but the most powerful piece on the board is the queen. She can move all over the board, much freer to influence the game than any other piece. She can also take on the movements and persona of a Rook, or Pawn, or Bishop—she can be protector and defender, a servant or a rule-maker. It's difficult to win a game of chess without your queen. It can be done, but its not easy.

The Queen of Wands

The Queen of Wands is the embodiment of the element of Fire. She influences events directly. Think Lioness. She can be any of the Fire signs, Aries, Leo or Sagittarius, or simply a women who embodies Fire qualities. She is not shy. She like the chase and a good challenge, and likes to tackle things head-on. Just like her counterpart The King of Wands, she impulsively acts first and thinks about it later. She is charismatic and attractive and always has lots of followers and fans. She's strong and determined to get what she wants when she wants it. She is not usually duplicitous, but she can flout rules and conventions when it suits her. She is exciting, warm, attractive and independent. She has no problem with face-to-face confrontations and is a little short on tact. She is energetic, smart, busy and active. She is usually sexy and a bit of a flirt. She is a natural leader, or rather, people follow her. She gets things done. She frequently has red hair.

The Queen of Cups

The Queen of Cups is the element of water personified. Think Mermaid. She may be a Pisces, Cancer or Scorpio woman, but not always. She is completely guided by her feelings in whatever she says and does. Her interactions are seldom direct so she influences events indirectly. She is a sweet, loving, sensitive creature who is seldom impulsive or impatient. She is dreamy and poetic and frequently musical. Some call her unrealistic, but she does shy away from direct confrontation and in this way she is a bit passive aggressive. She can usually be found in one of the creative professions or spending her days caring for others. She is a natural empath and instinctively senses emotional undercurrents. Her intuition is more important to her than being practical or conventional—she prefers to live in her own world. She avoids uncomfortable situations, physically or mentally, and would rather escape, using whatever means she has at her disposal.

COURT CARDS

The Queen of Swords

I like to call the Queen of Swords the 'Mother-in-Law card' because she frequently represents the stereo-typical personality type. She is usually a critical or bossy female in the querents reading. This Queen is hard to please. She has high standards and expects everyone in her world to meet them. She represents the element of Air, intellect over feelings. She is also often a divorced woman or a widow. She might be an Aquarius, Gemini or Libra woman. Her presence in a reading might also indicate a moment when the querent (if the querent is female) needs to take on those qualities to be effective in the given situation. She seems composed and stern on the outside, but she has deep feelings she seldom shows. She is not the kind of woman you mess with and get away with it. If she isn't happy, she can take your head off and never bat an eye. Then she can walk away, head high, and you will never see her again. She needs facts and details, and needs to thoroughly examine an issue before acting. She knows she can use knowledge and information to control.

She is intellectual rather than emotional. She can be forthright, almost to the point of abruptness, and lives to catch her adversaries off guard. It's best not to beat around the bush with her. She's up-front and honest and expects the same from others.

The Queen of Discs
The Queen of Discs or Coins (or Pentacles) represents the element of earth. She can be a Taurus, Virgo or Capricorn, or a wife and mother, boss or property owner of any sign. She represents solid, stable womanhood. She is welcoming, nurturing and homey. She handles every day matters in a sensible and practical way. She is usually good with business, especially Real Estate, and she doesn't have time for drama or silliness. She usually knows her way around a kitchen and can feed and take care of those she loves. When her people are happy, she's happy. She is usually warm, generous and happy herself, especially when her home is filled with friends, kids, noise, plants, animals and food. If something needs do-

ing, she does it without complaint. She is down-to-earth, loyal, practical and steadfast. She is everyone's mother.

THE KNIGHTS

Knights are young men or implied forward movement. They can be our son's, their friends, our brothers, our neighbors or co-workers. They themselves are always moving forward. They have energy and drive, are reckless, demanding and often immature. Knights like to adjust their environment to suit themselves. They are younger than Kings in disposition and maturity, if not actual age. A Knight can represent a specific younger male, (though older men may act like Knights), or even a boyish female. Knights can be pushy, self-centered and brash, without meaning to be. The horse is an important part of the Knight card, indicating a driving force moving events and situations forward, demanding progress at any cost.

There are scholars who attribute the Biblical four horsemen of the Apocalypse to the four suits of Knights. They designate the four horsemen as follows:

- Knight of Pentacles = Black Horse (Revelations 6:5), Function: To Determine
- Knight of Wands = Sandy Horse (Revelations 6:4),
    Function: To Battle
- Knight of Cups = Pale Horse (Revelations 6:8), Function: To Cut Down
- Knight of Swords = White Horse (Revelations 6:2),
    Function: To Conquer

In the Tarot, all the Knights have two meanings. Begin by assuming the Knight is an actual person. If that doesn't fit, consider that he is bringing you the qualities of the suit. Also be sure to watch what direction the horse is coming: towards you or away from you. If he is coming towards you or towards the other cards, the movement is coming towards you as well. If the horse is moving away from the other cards, it is an indication of movement away from you. See? It's simple.

The Knight of Wands

Like all Wands Court Cards, Knights also act first and think later. He's athletic, impatient and impulsive. He would rather initiate any action, even

COURT CARDS

a wrong one, than wait. Waiting is torture for this knight. He might be an Aries, Leo, or Sagittarius young man, but not always. His card is traditionally shown with flames (fire as a metaphor for speed) and he and his horse are usually in the process of climbing a mountain. He puts very little thought into long term strategy, but rushes into things without considering the consequences of his actions or their effect on others. He's focused on victory, glory and being the best. He can also be pushy, aggressive and highly insistent. He has no patience or tolerance who stand in his way or criticize his methods. This is also the card of creativity immediate action and sudden inspiration. It may indicate an event entering your life quickly and unexpectedly, or leaving just as fast, depending on which way his horse is charging.

The Knight of Cups

The Knight of Cups is a sensitive guy, with a huge imagination. He is the epitome of the element of Water. He is a true romantic. His head is frequently in the clouds, but he's intelligent and talented, too, possibly a poet, musician, or artist. He may be a Pisces, Cancer or Scorpio, but not always. This Knight is an angst-ridden dreamer. He prefers his own fantasy to everyone else's reality. He can be jealous, introspective, brooding and melodramatic. He is a lover of beauty and romance, less fond of practical considerations and day-to-day responsibilities. He craves change. He's over-sensitive and easily offended and can be shallow and inconsistent. He lives in illusion, intuition, obsession, sensuality, temptation, elusiveness and impermanence. If you are female, this card may foretell attention from an admirer, possibly younger. He may sweep you off your feet with pretty words and nothing to support them.

The Knight of Swords

The Knight of Swords is a young man who believes in his own intelligence. He uses sharp words, quick thinking and boundless mental energy to achieve his aims. He may be a Libra, Gemini, or Aquarius young man, or one who possesses those qualities. He charges forward ready to slay anyone in his way, or better yet, anyone who disagrees with him, and he's as likely to slay with his words as any weapon. He's creative, but in a clever, brainiac sort of way. He has no regard to the danger he faces as he charges forward or who he hurts in the process. Once his mind is made up, there's no stopping him. He pays no attention to risks or challenges, because he intends to win. He is often blinded by his need to be right at all costs. His difficulty lies in his blindness to responsibility and compassion. This Knight has great ambition and determination. The Knight of Swords can also let us know of an intellectual or verbal situation rushing towards you or moving away from you, and the challenge will be mental.

The Knight of Discs

The Knight of Discs represents a young man who is not afraid of work or responsibility. He is the only Knight who just sits on his horse, not moving forward. He can be Taurus, Virgo or Capricorn or someone else as earthy. This young man is the one who stops to do the necessary routine work, while

COURT CARDS

the other Knights charge away. In fact, he finds comfort in ordinary routine. He's willing to take his time. If he wants something, he's prepared to work for it and he doesn't mind biding his time. He is often considered a little boring by his peers, but that doesn't bother him—he smiles on his way to the bank. The Knight of Discs is more methodical than the other Knights. He's patient and reliable. He can be meticulous, steadfast, protective pragmatic, functional, industrious and quite a bit materialistic. He can be very attached to family. In a reading, This Knight can also foretell a new job, work project or opportunity coming towards you. Be certain everything is planned carefully. Take care of the details to ensure success, and don't take risks. Embrace the conservative and conventional tried and true methods and don't leave the job half done.

COURT CARDS

THE PAGES

Pages most often represent your children or the children in your life, brothers, sisters, neighbors or friends. Also Pages can foretell messages. Some Tarot decks use a princess in place of the page to represent a young girl. In your readings, a Page can represent a specific young person male or female, or anyone or anything with a message for us.

I like to think of a Page as a young person holding a fat satin pillow. On this pillow is a letter, which he brings to the King and Queen, sitting on their thrones. Picture the Knights standing to either side of the King and Queen. The page can either be the young person bringing the message or the actual message.

If a Page appears in a reading and no children seem to be involved (for example: the person you are reading for is childless, has no friends with kids, etc.), then a Page is a message. Whether it's a text, phone call, email, visit, or even a dream, a message is on the way.

Page of Wands
The Page of Wands is a free spirit. They are active, athletic, and usually creative and talented children. They can also be impetuous and flamboyant, maybe a little hyperactive with poor impulse control. They are the adventurers.

Or, as a message, it indicates communication about a course of action. Wands often foretell travel as well as passion and temper. This card can signify a message from far away about a trip, career move, or leadership position. When drawn with The Empress card, it could signify pregnancy.

Page of Cups
The Pages of Cups are the sweetest children in the Tarot. They are deep, calm, gentle and caring. They are often artistic. They can also be gullible, dreamy and sensitive. They are emotional, can be

psychic, tend to be solitary and are often misunderstood.

On the other hand, if your Page of Cups is a message, you can expect a sweet or romantic letter, email or phone call from someone. Whatever the message is, it will put a smile on your face and a song in your heart.

Page of Swords
The Pages of Swords are the intellegent kids, the scarcastic smarty-pants who always have an answer. They are the ones who argue with their teachers when they're older. They have quick minds and quick words. They are the geniuses, the insightful children with an opinion and something to say. They are also the most tech-savvy.

Or, if your Page of Swords is a message, it will be a great idea, some kind of communication about an important legal document to sign, or it can be a message with a sharp criticism.

COURT CARDS

Page of Discs

The Pages of Discs are the kids with common sense. They are usually good with money, whether saving it or investing it. Sincere, naturally curious, friendly, and studious, they can be devoted to their families and are usually good caregivers. They are usually the ones who take care of their younger siblings.

If your Page of Discs is a message, it could indicate communication about work or money, or the beginning of an idea about work or money.

If a Court Card appears in a reading and we aren't sure who it represents in life, there is a way to get more information. Pull the Court Card out of the layout and lay it down as a significator. Collect all the other cards together and shuffle, shuffle, shuffle, asking 'Who is this?' Now lay the other cards down around the significator in whatever layout you choose. The Celtic Cross (see later) is good for this but it really doesn't matter which layout you choose. Look at the cards around the significator. This usually explains them.

Sometimes a querent who has traditionally been a Queen of Cups finds herself in a situation where she is required to act more like a Queen of Swords, so we will see the Queen of Swords in the spread. In this way the card represents another aspect of the querent.

THE MAJOR ARCANA

We study the Major Arcana (also called Higher Arcana) last because they are the deepest cards and the most important. Arcana means "secrets," so the Major Arcana cards are the "big secrets." These are the cards representing important milestones, major changes, events beyond our control and spiritual growth.

Jungian Therapy uses the twenty-two images from the Major Arcana to illustrate and represent the phases of our soul's growth. In Esoteric Astrology each card represents a phase on the path to the development of our soul. This is sometimes referred to as "The Fool's Journey."

THE MAJOR ARCANA

In studying the Tarot, we agree to accept the responsibility of this study consciously and of our own free will. We students agree to use the Tarot to further us on our own path. We become more responsible in our actions, because we are not oblivious. We have decided to be proactive about our actions and our life. We want to impact our lives, rather than allow life to impact us. If we begin our study of the Tarot with the assumption that all parties involved in conducting a reading want to do the right thing then, according to Rachel Pollack (Tarot writer and teacher), "Tarot helps you meet whatever comes in the best possible way."

THE FOOL (0)
"Leaping before looking."

Child-like innocence, enthusiasm, wonder and guilelessness. It is about stepping off a cliff into the unknown without watching where you are going. This could be a good thing, or a not-so-good thing. The card of blind faith and keeping things simple.

Beginning, spontaneity. Freedom, risk, faith. Apparent folly. A new phase or path, the unexpected.

Letting go of expectations. Doing something just for the fun of it, with no thought to the consequences.

THE MAGICIAN (or THE ALCHEMIST) (I)
"Turning lead into gold."

The action/creativity principle. Become an alchemist. This card is about creating miracles, the ability to make something out of nothing. The Magician can and does utilize all elements of every suit. It's a reminder to trust in your own power to manifest. This is also the card of the artist.

Concentration. Power. Art. Will power. Making plans.

THE HIGH PRIESTESS (II)
"Take the spiritual path."

The passive principle. You can always find a higher road. Be a spiritual and moral example. Also, you may abstain from something, perhaps physical contact or sex, at least for a while.

Choose the spiritual path. Unconscious awareness, stillness. Non-action. Mystery, wisdom, spirituality. Creativity, intuition, celibacy.

THE EMPRESS (III)
"Celebrate the feminine."

The feminine principle. This card blesses the family. It reminds us of the importance of nurturing energy and the power of a comfortable home. This is the card of motherhood, but in an elevated, 'Divine Goddess' sort of way. Think about your favorite Thanksgiving Day. Visualize all those that you love sitting down to an abundant table to eat food lovingly prepared by you. That is the feeling of this card.

Home. Family matters. Motherhood, birth, cooking. Nurturing, abundance. Nature. Indulging the senses. Love, passion. Work with children.

THE EMPEROR (1V)
"That which rules us."

The masculine principle. Authority. A powerful organization. Have you filed your taxes yet? Are you indebted to the bank? Are you a student at a large university? Under your father's thumb? Are you an employee of a big corporation? This card forces us to be mindful of the people and organizations in our lives who exist as powerful, demanding entities. You need to deal with one of those organizations or an authority figure right now. This card insists we acknowledge their occasional control over us.

Fatherhood, authority. A powerful organization. Honor, structure. Reason rules over emotion. Authority. Regulation.

THE HIEROPHANT (or THE POPE) (V)
"Follow the rules."

This is the card of traditional values, events and rules. Marriage, church, ministers, going to a wedding or getting married is represented by this card. Sometimes the advice is to "follow the rules" or "focus on marriage."

Conservative values. Tradition and structure. Organized religion, spiritual blessings. Marriage, fatherhood. Education, belief systems. Conformity, society. Church, group identification.

THE LOVERS (VI)
"A significant relationship."

This card generally does not signify casual dating. It represents a serious love affair or relationship, something ground breaking, earth shaking, lasting, or at the very least, karmic and important. Or it could be that the querentit perceives the relationship as very important. This card suggests strongly that you pay attention to the love in your environment. It could be more important than you think. Or, this card may represent a difficult choice between two very tempting things.

A deep and meaningful relationship. Meant to be. Love, sexuality, relationship. Compelling attraction.

A choice between two pleasures. Sex, making love.

THE CHARIOT (VII)
"Moving forward."

This is card represents important movement, a trip, a relocation, or an important shift from one direction to another, but no matter the direction it is surely about moving forward. It is the opposite of stagnation. This card can represent actual vehicles like cars or planes. Also, it encourages us to work as a team, which brings greater rewards than working solo.

Travel, movement, transportation, will. Self-assertion, hard control. Working in tandem for a common cause. Winning, Choose a path.

STRENGTH (VIII)

"Gentleness triumphs over aggression."

Considered one of the best cards, powerful and good.

Stay strong: someone needs your help. Remain gentle in the face of force. This card represents an energy so powerful it triumphs over any and all aggression. It is the card of strength, but not force. In fact, this card is the opposite of force. It represents the power of internal strength and force of character. Gently refuse to yield. Hold your ground, because you are right. Do not let a bully win. This is also an indicator that you may be given an opportunity to help someone in need.

Quiet strength and patience transform negativity. Compassion, soft control.

THE HERMIT (IX)
"Solitude and introspection."

This is the card of aloneness. It signifies a quiet time of contemplation and possibly study. You need to be alone. Please do not resort to enforced socialization to fill the silence; your answer is in the silence. Allow this time to enrich your soul and mind.

Quiet and solitude. Teaching. Wisdom, guidance, maturity. Study in private. A current or extended period of alone time. Searching. Living alone.

WHEEL OF FORTUNE (X)
"Taking a risk."

This card represents a gamble. It reminds us that sometimes we just have to risk it without the certainty of an outcome. That's the thing about gambling: sometimes when you take a chance you win big, sometimes you don't. Destiny, fate, luck, karma. Take a chance, throw the dice.

Turning point, a change of fortune. Risk, gambling. No guarantee.

JUSTICE (XI)

"The (universal) legal system."

This card represents fairness, justice, courts, and the law. It can be a reminder to pay close attention to legal documents. This card is also a call to restore balance and do the right thing. It may be reminding you to right a wrong.

Truth, justice, honesty. Cause and effect. Decision, moral choice. The law, the legal system. Fairness, a just outcome. Important legal documents.

THE HANGED MAN (XII)
"Let go. There's nothing you can do."

Sometimes, the best action is no action. Sometimes things are simply out of our control and the more we try to change them the more they slip away from us. Step back. Let go of any attachment to an outcome. The more peace you can find in the situation without trying to influence it, the happier you will be. There is nothing you can do to influence the outcome so stop trying.

Sacrifice, accepting what is. Reversal, detachment. Letting go, martyrdom.

DEATH (XIII)
"An ending."

This card signifies the end of something. Take care of any unfinished business and let go. It's over. This card can also represent a new life but just the beginning, because something has to end first. It does not usually signify an actual death unless it is next to the Ten of Swords and/or Three of Hearts or The Tower. New brides frequently get The Death card in readings, and it represents the end of their single status.

Transition. Elimination. Inexorable forces moving towards an ending. Let go, something needs to end. Going through what cannot be avoided.

TEMPERANCE (XIV)

"Moderation in all things."

This is usually an advice card, recommending you practice moderation and balance. For some reason only you can know, this is particularly difficult for you right now. Slow down or speed up, let go of excessive habits or behaviors. Stay centered. Regain your balance. Stop drinking so much. Stop working so much. Get more sleep. Resist excess of any kind.

Temperance, calm, balance. Moderation, equilibrium.

Mixing things up. Health, sobriety, walking the middle road. Avoid excesses.

THE MAJOR ARCANA

THE DEVIL (XV)

"Obsession!"

The opposite of the Temperance card. You are becoming obsessed! Obsessions come in all forms and can fool us into thinking we are behaving in a rational manner. This card lets you know that something is very wrong and it needs change. You may be fooling yourself but you are not fooling the cards. Something or someone is worrying you excessively, endangering you or you are obsessing and it is getting in your way.

Allowing this situation to continue leaves no room for you to access any divine inspiration, energy or grace. Feeding attachments is indicated with this card, and not in a good way. Get back to your spiritual center: pray, meditate, go see your therapist, quit worrying about money, sage your house. Your physical world is making you crazy. This is the card of bad relationships, sometimes abusive or obsessive, or bondage to someone or something.

Conquer your demons. Excessive worry, especially about money. Materialism. Low desires or beliefs. Sex, bondage, illusions, bad decisions made knowingly. Allowing control. Dark secrets, hidden evil.

THE TOWER (XVI)
"Shock and awe."

Expect the unexpected when you draw this card. The shock could be a good thing, or a not-so-good thing. But no matter how you view it or how you prepare for it, you will still be unsettled. Expect the unexpected. Exciting news. Shock and awe!

Sudden change. Upheaval. Downfall, revelation, a shocking discovery. Reversal of fortune, chaos, a crisis. A flash of insight.

THE STAR (XVII)
"A shining star."

This is a special card. It signifies hope and inspiration, flashes of blinding insight, and stardom. It's time to fine-tune your cause and develop your fan base so your people have something important to follow. Have faith in your path; it is the right one. Follow your muse. Stop hiding your own light and allow it to shine. It is time to embrace the grandest version of yourself. You are a star.

Public acclaim, recognition. Faith, hope, inspiration.

THE MOON (XVIII)
"The answer cannot be known at this time."

Either there is a mystery about the situation, or we do not get to know the answer right now. This is the card of the mystical, the things not seen with the naked eye. Something is hidden from you for a reason; you should probably stop asking about it.

You don't get to know. Instinct, imagination, secrets. Fear, illusion, mystery. Strong dreams, premonitions. Phobias, deception.

THE SUN (XIX)
"It's a great day."

This card is one of the happiest cards in the deck. The sun is shining, the birds are singing, the baby is smiling, everyone is content. It's a great time to be alive so take advantage of it, and be sure to say "Thank you."

Good news. Abundance, contentment. Enlightenment. Greatness, clarity. Vitality, freedom, happiness, understanding. Prominence, enthusiasm. Good health, brightness.

JUDGEMENT (XX)

"A new beginning, after an ending."

Recently something ended. In some of the older tarot decks this card was called "Resurrection" and it represents a fresh start, a new life after a death of sorts. This should encourage us to have confidence in a new life direction and a new, more meaningful way of life.

Judgment, rebirth. Inner calling, big change. Absolution, taking a stand. Restored relationship after hardship. Hard choices, a fresh start.

THE WORLD (XXI)
"On top of the world!"

This is the last card in the deck and the best. Getting this card in your future trumps all the other cards in your reading and it tells you no matter what other cards are around you, the world is your oyster. Everything you have worked for is yours. It is big achievement, real accomplishment, and true mastery.

Success, fulfillment. Accomplishment, a great understanding. Public acclaim, realizing goals. Finding a beautiful solution.

SPREADS

A spread is another word for laying your Tarot cards in a specific order, with each position representing a different meaning or area of your life. A spread can be as simple as one to three cards or all of them, laid out in rows. Some spreads are classically traditional (like The Celtic Cross, see later in this chapter) or quirky and new. The most important thing to remember about the spread you choose to use is its ease of use and meaning for you. I like to start new readers off with three card spreads. They are simple, versatile, and can be easily customized.

Three Card Tarot Spreads

Three-card Tarot spreads are great if you need a quick answer to an uncomplicated question, or are just learning to read the cards. If you want to practice with a number of fast Tarot spreads and readings, these are the best. Even for the seasoned Tarot reader, a three-card Tarot reading can often give you all the info you need about a subject, and help you get back to basics. They serve as a reminder that even the most complex situations can have simple answers.

Here are a number of easy three-card Tarot spreads to get you started. Feel free to mix and match between the suggestions below to create your own three-card Tarot spreads. You will discover a few favorites to use time and time again. Just be sure to decide which spread you will be using before you shuffle and throw the cards.

Understanding a Situation

- Past / Present / Future
- What will help you / Hinder you / What's your unrealized potential
- The nature of your problem / The cause / The solution
- Current situation / Obstacle / Advice
- Situation / Action / Outcome
- Context of the situation / Where you need to focus / Outcome
- What you think about the situation / What you feel / What you do
- Where you stand now / What you aspire to / How to get there
- What you aspire to / What's standing in your way / How you can overcome this
- What you can change / Can't change / What you may not be aware of
- What worked well / Did not work well / Key learnings

Understanding Relationships
- You / The other person / The relationship
- What you want from the relationship / What they want from the relationship / Where the relationship is heading
- What brings you together / Pulls you apart / Needs your attention

Making Choices and Decisions
- Strengths / Weaknesses / Advice
- Opportunities / Challenges / Outcome
- Option 1 / Option 2 / Option 3
- Option 1 / Option 2 / What you need to know to make a decision
- The solution / An alternative solution / How to choose

Understanding Yourself
- Mind / Body / Spirit
- Your conscious mind / Subconscious mind / Superconscious mind
- Material state / Emotional state / Spiritual state

- You / Your current path / Your potential
- Stop / Start / Continue
- What the Universe wants you to be / Personal qualities required / Specific action required

Past / Present / Future

This is the classic three card spread beloved by many readers for good reason.

Do This / Don't Do This / Overview

An easy way to get insight on a perplexing situation, or one in which there are many possible actions.

Choice 1 / Choice 2 / Situation

When there are two ways to go, and you need help in making your decision.

Problem / Background / Advice

Good for a tricky situation, and also for a daily spread.

Mind / Body / Spirit

Also good for a daily spread. Can be used in two ways: (a) What your mind, body, spirit need, or (b) What you're thinking about, what you need, what will set you free.

What you know / What you do not know / Advice

Good for making sure.

Blessings: From yourself / From your loved ones / From Spirit

This can be an encouraging spread. Try it when you're feeling down.

The first card indicates the blessings you bring to yourself. The next card shows the blessings your friends and families are bringing you now. The last cards are those blessings coming to you from outside.

The Story

This spread differs from most others in that the card positions themselves have no specific meaning. Instead, you place the cards any way you like so that the cards read like a narrative. This is a truly intuitive reading.

A great yes/no spread.

I learned this from Tarot 'High Priestess' Barbara Moore and it can completely organize a yes/no question.

First, remove the 'Wheel of Fortune' card and set it aside, face down. Now, formulate your question. It must be a clear "Yes/No" question. Now hold it in your mind, even repeat it over and over while you mix your cards. Now remove seven cards in any order you choose while repeating your question. Place these cards face down on top of your Wheel of Fortune card and put the rest of your deck away. Take the eight remaining cards (The Wheel of Fortune plus the pulled seven cards) and mix, face down of course.

Now lay them out like this:

Definitely yes   Probably yes
Card one / Card two   Card three / Card four

Definitely no   Probably no
Card five / Card six   Card seven / Card eight

The group of two containing the 'Wheel of Fortune' card is the answer. But when you read the cards in both yes and no groups, you get the 'Why?' and 'Why not?' Really fun!

A word about Significators.

Many Tarot readers use Significators. They are a card chosen by the reader to signify the querent in a reading, like a placeholder. I do not. I often don't know the person I'm reading for well enough to make a choice of card. I find if its important for them to know who they are in the tarot their card will show up, sometimes in the first card thrown down in the place a significator would be.

SPREADS

I like to get to the meat of the reading as quickly as possible, so I don't use a significator. I think the first card thrown after I have the querent shuffle is an important one. Sometimes it's enlightening and sets the pace for the whole reading. If a court card pops up, I describe them so the querent can see if they sound familiar. Then we can assign them to someone known, and if not, someone to look for.

If we aren't sure who we are talking about, I pull out the Court Card; lay it down as a significator and shuffle, shuffle, shuffle, asking 'who is this?' And I look at the cards around them. This usually explains them. Or, sometimes a querent who has traditionally been a Queen of Cups' finds herself as in a situation where she is required to act more like a Queen of swords.

I don't like to limit myself in my readings. But, you may really enjoy learning reverse meanings. Like I always say, it's your deck of cards and your readings—-do what you want.

SPREADS

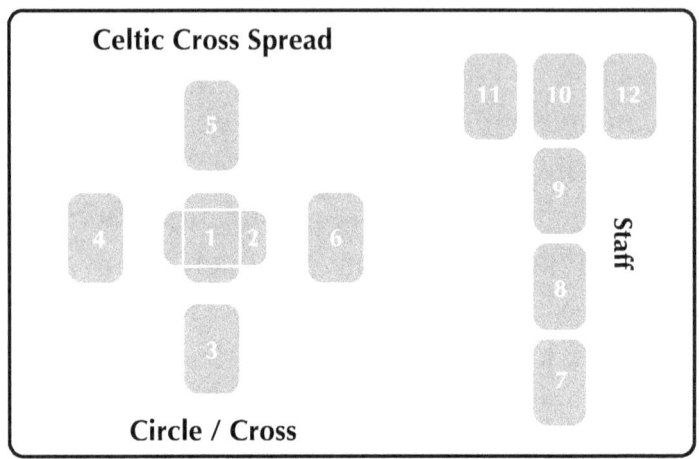

Some thoughts on the Celtic Cross layout.

A diagram of the classic Celtic Cross layout seems to be required in every Tarot book known to man. The problem is, the positions and meanings all seem to contradict each other. Some say use a Significator, others put three cards in the center as number one, and one result card at the end. It is really fascinating how different the classic Celtic Cross can be. That's why it is such a great tool. Just remember, Tarot means something different to every reader. I do it differently than any others I have seen, and I cannot tell you how it happened, or why. I only know it works for me. I will include it here, but please feel free to mix it up to suit yourself.

Card one—The situation

Card two—What is covering the situation

Card three—Where you are with the situation right now

Card four—The past

Card five—What you are thinking about, what is on your mind

Card six—The step to the answer

Card seven—Your negative feelings on the subject

Card eight—Your friends and family, your immediate environment

Card nine—Your positive feelings on the subject

Card ten — The answer

I like to do two more cards in addition to card ten, call them cards eleven and twelve (one on each side of ten). Cards eleven and twelve are meant to describe card ten.

Then I do something weird. I start laying cards one after another right under the cross and I keep going until I hit a Major Arcana card, and then I

SPREADS

count the number of cards until the Major Arcana card and that is the number of days weeks, or months until the resolution. If a Major Arcana card is the first card out down there, I know the solution is at hand. If it seems like it keeps going and going without a Major Arcana card, it is an ongoing situation without an easy resolution. And these cards themselves tell their own story, much like a storyboard for a movie.

Ok, so here's an easy way to use the cards when you don't have a table, or room to spread out your cards. Shuffle, shuffle shuffle. Cut. Look at the cards on the bottom of each stack. Pull them out and off to the side, side by side. Shuffle shuffle, shuffle. Cut. Take the bottom cards from each stack of cards again and place the first under your first card and the second under the second. Do it again. Keep doing this until you get a Major Arcana card on each side, then stop. Say the key words for each card in succession, like a narrative. Or, move them around until the story they tell makes sense to you.

SPREADS

I've done this in the passenger seat on a long road trip and in the back of a tour bus. Entertaining.

A word about reading reversed, inverted or upside down cards.

I do not read inverted cards, and never did. If a card comes out upside down in a reading I straighten it out and keep going. I started doing this when I was first learning because Tarot meanings were confusing enough without adding reverse descriptions and alternate meanings. Some of my Tarot students went on to learn and use reversed meanings and I love them for that. In my version of beginners Tarot classes, we do not read reversed cards. I'm all about keeping it simple at this stage, and I feel trying to learn reversed meanings as well complicates the learning process unnecessarily. As you get more proficient you are welcome to add them later if you want. You may really enjoy learning reverse meanings. Remember, it's your deck of cards and your reading: do what you want.

A FINAL WORD

I was handed my first deck of Tarot cards after a funeral. The day was dark, the death was dark (the accidental drug overdose of a close friend's husband) and we were trying to clean out the house. My friend found the deck of cards in her husband's closet and gave them to me. Little did I know, the gift of these cards compelled my life to take an unexpected turn.

tricky deck for a beginner to learn to say the least, but I persisted. I still own the six or seven books on the Crowley Deck I studied trying to master it. But I never felt the Thoth Deck was 'my' deck. I wasn't 'in love' with it (an important piece of the

A FINAL WORD

Tarot reading puzzle) and I'm still not a big fan of Aleister Crowley. But by the time I realized all of this I was hooked on the Tarot.

I switched to Rider-Waite based Tarot decks, which were easier for me to read because of the illustrations on every card, but still confusing to try to learn on my own. My current favorite deck and the one I recommend to all new readers now is 'The Golden Tarot' by Kat Black' I acquired quite a library of books on the Tarot searching for the definitive one. And I kept buying more books.

You see, most Tarot books are complicated. I think some of their authors believe their books have to be complicated because the Tarot itself is so deep. It seems Tarot books always include every conceivable meaning for each card and combinations of cards. Only the most gifted reader can possibly be expected to memorize them all and be intuitive at the same time.

It took me years of practice to feel comfortable enough to read Tarot cards for other people and

A FINAL WORD

many more years before I realized the truth about the Tarot: it's actually quite simple. And the simpler you keep it the better it works.

Reading the Tarot is never about other people's meanings for the cards. The Tarot is fluid and adaptable, and conforms to our own unique feelings about each card, so learning it means understanding the meanings you assign to them. Because that fact is the most important aspect to reading, I suggest getting to that place as quickly as possible. That's why I wrote this book: I wrote the book I wish I could have found when I was starting to read the Tarot.

If you read my Tarot Primer first, before any other Tarot book confuses you, it can get you reading your Tarot cards in about three hours. After you get the hang of it, go ahead and read all those other great Tarot books. Knock yourself out. Expand and explore your knowledge, and get really, really good. But for now, we start with the basics.

Good luck!

NOTES

NOTES

NOTES

Deborah Carter Mastelotto

Deborah is a pathological entrepreneur, an obsessive remodeler, a minor student of quantum physics, an unapologetic observer of human nature and an indefatigable advice-giver. And she has a lovely little salon called Pink West in a hundred-year-old farm house in Dripping Springs, Texas.

Visit: Pinkchronicity.com & Pinkwestsalon.com